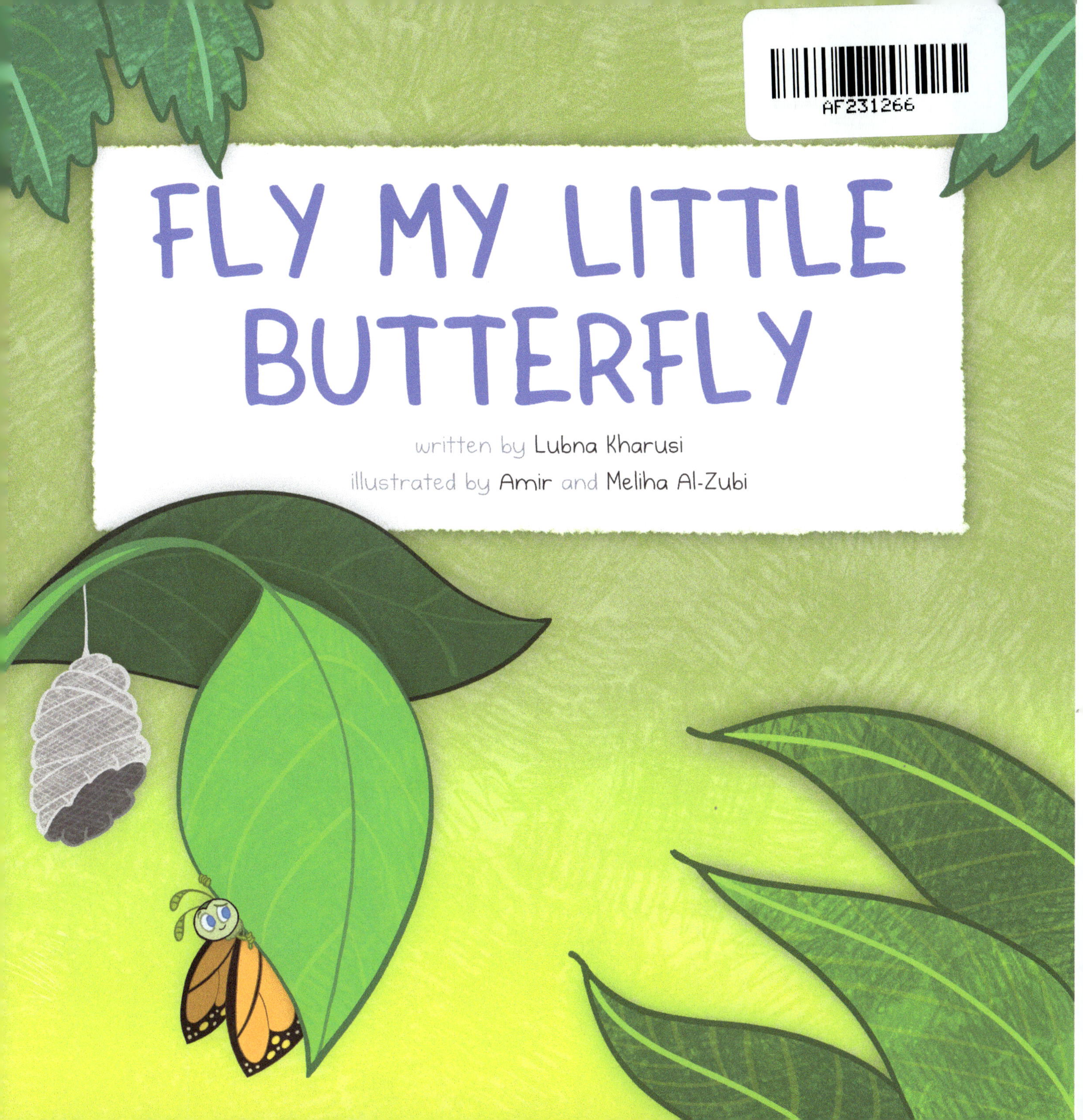

AF231266
FLY MY LITTLE BUTTERFLY
written by Lubna Kharusi
illustrated by Amir and Meliha Al-Zubi

Published by
Lubybuby 483 Green Lanes,
London, N13 4BS, UK,
www.lubybuby.com
ISBN 978-0-9930901-2-7 Fly my little Buttefly

This book is dedicated to my little girls Aya and Khair.

As a parent, the most important gift we can give to our children is self esteem and the confidence to go out into the world believing in themselves and their capacity to live their full potential.

We are all on this earth to fulfill a purpose, and it is only through trusting our intuition that we can achieve our individualised mission.

We are diverse creations, and what is true for one person may not be true for another. Let us give our children the freedom and confidence to discover what is right for them, to believe and trust who they are, and not be limited to other people's perceptions of who they can be.

This book contains values and wisdom that parents may want to share with their children to prepare them for the world.

Lubna Kharusi

FLY MY LITTLE BUTTERFLY
THERE IS NO NEED TO BE SHY

YOU DON'T NEED TO EXPLAIN WHY
SPREAD YOUR WINGS UP IN THE SKY

SING MY LITTLE PEACEFUL BIRD
MAKE THE DIFFERENCE WITH YOUR WORDS

DON'T BE AFRAID TO BE HEARD
WHAT YOU SAY CAN CHANGE THE WORLD

EXPLORE MY LITTLE BUMBLEBEE
BEAUTY'S EVERYWHERE TO SEE

LET YOUR SPIRIT WONDER FREE
LIVE ALWAYS WITH JOY AND GLEE

ALWAYS BE TRUE MY LITTLE PONY
THERE'S NO NEED TO BE A PHONEY

IT MAY BE TEMPTING WHEN YOU'RE LONELY
STAY PROUD OF WHO YOU ARE MY PONY

LOOK AROUND MY LITTLE BUNNY
THERE'S ALWAYS SOMETHING THAT IS FUNNY

DON'T RUSH THROUGH LIFE IN A HURRY
ALL WORKS OUT IN THE END, DON'T WORRY

STAND TALL MY LITTLE GIRAFFE
FOCUS AND BELIEVE IN YOUR PATH

NO ONE ELSE CAN DO YOUR MATH
DON'T LIVE YOUR LIFE ON OTHERS' BEHALF

PERSEVERE MY LITTLE ANT
DON'T BELIEVE THOSE WHO SAY YOU CAN'T

APPROACH A PROBLEM WITH A SLANT
WATCH YOUR SEEDS GROW INTO PLANTS

SHARE YOUR THINGS MY LITTLE SEAL
HELP THE OTHERS HAVE A MEAL

BY GIVING FREELY, JOY YOU'LL FEEL
THIS REWARD IS THE ULTIMATE DEAL

CAREFUL MY LITTLE FOX, BE KIND
THAT LITTLE MOUSE ON WHICH YOU DINE

CAN BE YOUR FRIEND THAT FREES YOUR MIND
DON'T ATTACK, GIVE IT A LITTLE TIME

MY LITTLE LION IT'S OK TO CRY
WHAT'S IMPORTANT IS THAT YOU TRY

FEELINGS ARE THINGS YOU CANNOT BUY
LET THEM OUT AND FEEL THE HIGH

ALWAYS FORGIVE MY LITTLE KITTEN
EVEN THE PUPPY BY WHICH YOU WERE BITTEN

ONE DAY YOU TWO MAY BE SMITTEN
EVERY RULE CAN BE REWRITTEN

TRUST YOUR INSTINCTS LITTLE BEAR
LISTEN TO YOUR HEART AND SNIFF THE AIR

SOMETHINGS MAY SEEM TOO BIG TO BARE
YOU WILL KNOW WHEN IT'S TIME TO DARE.

ENJOY THE OCEAN MY LITTLE FISH
THE WORLD IS HERE TO GRANT YOUR WISH

THOUGHTS CAN BE REAL IN JUST A SWISH
BELIEVE YOU WILL BE SERVED YOUR DISH

LOVE EVERYONE MY LITTLE FAWN
THIS IS WHY YOU HAVE BEEN BORN

DON'T LET FEAR BECOME YOUR NORM
LIGHT UP THE WORLD LIKE THE DAWN.

Purchase our other AMAZING BOOKS!
Download free Music & Videos from www.lubybuby.com
lubybuby©
WORDS AND IDEAS THAT CAN CHANGE THE WORLD
Made of Love
by Lubna Kharusi
ILLUSTRATED BY: Amir AND Meliha Al-Zubi
MUSIC BY: Hakely Nakao Chavez, Thanae Pachiyannakis AND Lubna Kharusi
Lubna Kharusi
I AM PERFECT
illustrated by Amir and Meliha Al-Zubi
music by Rene Gomez Sanchez, Thanae Pachiyannakis and Lubna Kharusi
Lubna Kharusi
I LOVE YOU MORE THAN...
Picture Dictionary
Aa
ILLUSTRATIONS BY Amir AND Meliha Al-Zubi
www.lubybuby.cor